FRANCIS FRITH'S
TOWN&**CITY**
MEMORIES

BURNLEY

The late KEN BOLTON lived in the Burnley area all his life except for his war service in the RAF. He was a development engineer at Rolls Royce in Barnoldswick until he joined the staff of Burnley Technical College in 1959. Sadly, Ken died in 2005.

Also Burnley born, ROGER FROST is a graduate of Manchester University and a former teacher and lecturer. He has many local history titles to his credit, and he writes a weekly column in the Burnley Express.

Ken and Roger worked together on several local history projects, most notably on 'Burnley Revisited', which raised money for Hospice Care.

St James' Street c1955 B251024

FRANCIS FRITH'S
TOWN *&* **CITY**
MEMORIES

BURNLEY

KEN BOLTON & ROGER FROST

FRANCIS FRITH'S
TOWN & CITY
MEMORIES

First published as Burnley, A Photographic History of your Town
in 2002 by Black Horse Books, an imprint of The Francis Frith Collection
Revised edition published in the United Kingdom in 2006 by
The Francis Frith Collection as Burnley, Town and City Memories
Limited Hardback Edition ISBN 1-84589-130-9
Paperback Edition ISBN 1-84589-131-7

British Library Cataloguing in Publication Data

Burnley
Town and City Memories
Ken Bolton & Roger Frost

The Francis Frith Collection®
Frith's Barn, Teffont,
Salisbury, Wiltshire SP3 5QP
Tel: +44 (0) 1722 716 376
Email: info@francisfrith.co.uk
www.francisfrith.com

Aerial photographs reproduced under licence from Simmons Aerofilms Limited
Historical Ordnance Survey maps reproduced under licence from Homecheck.co.uk

Printed and bound in England

Front Cover: **BURNLEY, DUKE BAR 1906** 54183t
The colour-tinting in this image is for illustrative purposes only,
and is not intended to be historically accurate

FRANCIS FRITH'S

TOWN *&* CITY

MEMORIES

CONTENTS

FRANCIS FRITH, Victorian founder of the world-famous photographic archive, was a devout Quaker and a highly successful Victorian businessman. By 1860 he was already a multi-millionaire, having established and sold a wholesale grocery business in Liverpool. He had also made a series of pioneering photographic journeys to the Nile region. The images he returned with were the talk of London. An eminent modern historian has likened their impact on the population of the time to that on our own generation of the first photographs taken on the surface of the moon.

Frith had a passion for landscape, and was as equally inspired by the countryside of Britain as he was by the desert regions of the Nile. He resolved to set out on a new career and to use his skills with a camera. He established a business in Reigate as a specialist publisher of topographical photographs.

Frith lived in an era of immense and sometimes violent change. For the poor in the early part of Victoria's reign work was a drudge and the hours long, and ordinary people had precious little free time. Most had not travelled far beyond the boundaries of their own town or village. Mass tourism was in its infancy during the 1860s, but during the next decade the railway network and the establishment of Bank Holidays and half-Saturdays gradually made it possible for the working man and his family to enjoy holidays and to see a little more of the world. With characteristic business acumen, Francis Frith foresaw that these new tourists would enjoy having souvenirs to commemorate their days out. He began selling photo-souvenirs of seaside resorts and beauty spots, which the Victorian public pasted into treasured family albums.

Frith's aim was to photograph every town and village in Britain. For the next thirty years he travelled the country by train and by pony and trap, producing fine photographs of seaside resorts and beauty spots that were keenly bought by millions of Victorians.

THE RISE OF FRITH & CO

Each photograph was taken with tourism in mind, the small team of Frith photographers concentrating on busy shopping streets, beaches, seafronts, picturesque lanes and villages. They also photographed buildings: the Victorian and Edwardian eras were times of huge building activity, and town halls, libraries, post offices, schools and technical colleges were springing up all over the country. They were invariably celebrated by a proud Victorian public, and photo souvenirs – visual records – published by F Frith & Co were sold in their hundreds of thousands. In addition, many new commercial buildings such as hotels, inns and pubs were photographed, often because their owners specifically commissioned Frith postcards or prints of them for re-sale or for publicity purposes.

In order to gain some understanding of the scale of Frith's business one only has to look at the catalogue issued by Frith & Co in 1886: it runs to some 670 pages. By 1890 Frith had created the greatest specialist photographic publishing company in the world, with over 2,000 stockists! The picture on the right shows the Frith & Co display board on the wall of the stockist at Ingleton in the Yorkshire Dales (left of window). Beautifully constructed with a mahogany frame and gilt inserts, it displayed a dozen scenes.

POSTCARD BONANZA

The ever-popular holiday postcard we know today took many years to appear, and F Frith & Co was in the vanguard of its development. Postcards became a hugely popular means of communication and sold in their millions. Frith's company took full advantage of this boom and soon became the major publisher of photographic view postcards.

Francis Frith died in 1898 at his villa in Cannes, his great project still growing. His sons Eustace and Cyril continued their father's monumental task, expanding the number of views offered to the public and recording more and more places in Britain, as the coasts and countryside were opened up to mass travel. The archive Frith created continued in business for another seventy years. By 1970 it contained over a third of a million pictures of 7,000 cities, towns and villages. The massive photographic record Frith has left to us stands as a living monument to a special and very remarkable man.

This book shows Burnley as it was photographed by this world-famous archive at various periods in its development over the past 150 years. Every photograph was taken for a specific commercial purpose, which explains why the selection may not show every aspect of the town landscape. However, the photographs, compiled from one of the world's most celebrated archives, provide an important and absorbing record of your town.

INTRODUCTION

BURNLEY is an industrial and market town in the Lancashire Pennines. It was once the largest cotton-weaving town in the world and the centre of the loom-making industry, but now its almost 90,000 people are employed in a wide variety of industrial and commercial enterprises.

The town today is perhaps best known because of its famous football club, which, after a number of years in the sporting wilderness, is now enjoying success once more. There is, though, more to Burnley than 'the Clarets'. Burnley is a town with a distinctive history, and its links with its past, despite the effects of industrialisation, are still tangible.

Burnley is overlooked by moors and hills, and it is to these places that we have to turn if we are to understand Burnley's early development. To the east of the town there are numerous prehistoric sites mostly related to the burial practices of the Bronze Age; but of the Romans little remains, and of the Dark Ages hardly anything save place names survives.

Burnley does not appear in the Domesday Book of 1086. It is, however, likely that at this time there was a small village situated on the banks of the Brun (the river after which the town was named). We do know that in 1122 the church of Burnley (St Peter's, see 35790, opposite) was granted to the monks of Pontefract Priory in Yorkshire. Another grant, this time in 1294 by Edward I, established Burnley's weekly market. Two years later a water-powered fulling mill, for use in the woollen industry, was constructed. This joined the already existing water mill, which was later to be called the King's Soke Mill, the rightful place for the production of flour in what was the extensive manor of Ightenhill.

Even though Burnley contained all these facilities by the end of the 13th century, it remained only a vill of the manor of Ightenhill. It was not for another two hundred years or so that because of the decline in manorial government Burnley acquired its own local administration — meetings were held in the vestry of St Peter's.

In the 16th century Burnley continued to develop. It was then that the first shops were constructed in what is now Church Street. At that time the wool industry was becoming important, and by the end of the 18th century, the first signs of industrialisation can be identified. Water-powered mills were constructed or adapted from former corn mills, more mines were opened, and perhaps most

INTRODUCTION

ST PETER'S CHURCH 1895 35790

This is an unusual photograph of Burnley's parish church in that it is taken from the north, where the trees make photography difficult. The photographer has managed to get round this problem by making use of one of the upstairs windows of the Old Grammar School. St Peter's occupies the original site of the community that eventually became Burnley, which perhaps dates from the Dark Ages. This was a relatively easy position to defend because the river almost surrounds the site. We can see the Church Street Road Bridge to the left, and the land upon which the church is built slopes down quite steeply to the river. To the right of the tower stands St Peter's Church School, Burnley's oldest school.

tellingly of all, the Leeds and Liverpool Canal came to Burnley in the 1790s.

At that time another most important change was taking place. The whole of the shopping centre, together with the market, was moved to the relatively flat land of what is now St James' Street. In a relatively short space of time, Burnley became an industrial town of the first rank. Its main industry was cotton manufacturing, though coal mining and engineering were important.

This does not mean to say that Burnley has little to show other than industrial monuments. In fact there are a number of these (the Weaver's Triangle Visitor Centre and Queen Street Mill, for example), but Burnley is a most varied town. A great deal of its past has been preserved; the original market cross, the Shorey Well (at one time the only source of drinking water in the town), and the Cliviger stocks are but three examples. Burnley contains two country houses (Towneley and Gawthorpe, both open to the public), and the Borough has some very good parks, two of which have Green Flag status.

Of course, where the buildings have gone we are fortunate to have photographs of the quality that we are able to use in this book. We hope that this photographic history of your town brings back memories for those of you who recall the Burnley of old, and that it inspires others to consider their town in a different way.

TOP O' TH' TOWN

THOSE who lived in this part of Burnley in the past were proud of the fact. They called themselves Top o' th' Towners, and they looked down on those who lived at the Bottom o' th' Town, perhaps half a mile away. The two names are derived from the fact that in the Middle Ages Burnley had two centres of population. The Top o' th' Town, on the Brun, was the more important because it contained the church, the market and the school. The Bottom o' th' Town was situated on the River Calder perhaps a hundred yards from its confluence with the Brun.

The Top o' th' Town still retains some of the character of Old Burnley. The width of Church Street at its junction with Ormerod Road is a reminder that this was once the market place for the old town, but the dominant building remains St Peter's church. Superficially, St Peter's looks Victorian, and it is certainly true that the church was enlarged in the 1850s; but quite a lot of the earlier building survives. The lower part of the tower dates from the 15th century, part of the roof is from the reign of Henry VIII, and the south and north aisles are respectively 18th- and early 19th-century reconstructions. Internally, it is possible that some of the pillars are the original Norman ones tooled down.

ST PETER'S CHURCH, THE INTERIOR,
LOOKING EAST 1895 35792

This photograph shows how the church was extended in the 1850s — at this time there was great demand for pews in St Peter's. It would have been difficult to extend the building, because its site was constrained by the Brun, so the solution was to construct galleries. The Master window, in the middle, is dedicated to the memory of Robert Mosley Master: when he left Burnley after thirty years in 1855, he became Archdeacon of Manchester.

ST PETER'S CHURCH, SOUTH-WEST 1895 35791

A hint of the heavily-wooded banks of the Brun can be seen on the left of this picture. It was here, in what was called the 'steepland of St Peter's', that Burnley Grammar School was founded in 1559, though there had been a 'song school' at St Peter's many years before that. A flag flies from what is a wonderful vantage point, and the tower itself reminds us that St Peter's has a very good peal of bells.

TOP O' TH' TOWN

The pictures of the cannons (35801, below, and 35801x, page 14) were taken from the junction of Bank Parade, to the right, and Colne Road. The tip of what appears to be a tower obscured by trees is part of the former Burnley Grammar School, and between that building and the cannons are the Grammar School gardens. It was here that the old cockpit was sited.

There was traditional cock fighting in Burnley, but this cockpit was also the venue for an annual cockshy. The boys of the Grammar School claimed the right from their Headmaster, on the payment of a fine (which was part of his salary!), to organise a cockshy in which the birds were stoned to death, the last surviving bird being declared the winner.

COLNE ROAD AND THE RUSSIAN CANNONS 1895 35801

In the distance, on the right, is Bank Parade house, once the home of Sir James Mackenzie (1853-1925). He was a medical practitioner in Burnley, and became famous for his researches into diseases of the heart. A plaque on the building records his achievements. To the left we can see the roof of St Peter's. On the extreme right, the wall is that of the Bank Hall estate, the home of General the Hon Sir James Yorke Scarlett, the hero of Balaclava and the reason for the proximity of the Russian cannons.

TOP O' TH' TOWN

THE RUSSIAN CANNONS 1895 35801x

General Peel, then Secretary for War, presented the Russian cannons to Burnley in 1867. This seemingly unusual gift was made because of Burnley's associations with the Crimean War. The cannons were a popular feature of old Burnley, but unfortunately they were taken for scrap metal during the war effort in 1941.

Today nothing can be seen of the cockpit, but the gardens are most interesting — they contain some of Burnley's oldest relics, which are all associated with the Top o' th' Town area. The original market cross of 1294 (sometimes erroneously called the Paulinus Cross) is preserved here, and so is the base of the 17th-century market cross and also part of the original stocks at which generations of Burnley miscreants were punished and humiliated. Also within the gardens is the Shorey Well, which until 1819 was the only public source of water in the Top o' th' Town area.

The Old Grammar School (35802, below), which overlooks St Peter's, is one of Burnley's most impressive buildings. It dates from 1873, and is the work of the local architect William Waddington. To the left of the building are the trees of the Grammar School Gardens, and across Bank Parade, we can see the trees in the gardens of Brown Hill.

Continuing the educational theme, the last view in this part of town is of Burnley College (B251022, page 16-17) which is situated on Ormerod Road. It was built in 1909 to the designs of Burnley's Borough Engineer, Mr G H Pickles, and at one time it served as the Municipal College and School of Art as well as the Burnley High School for Girls.

THE OLD GRAMMAR SCHOOL 1895 35802

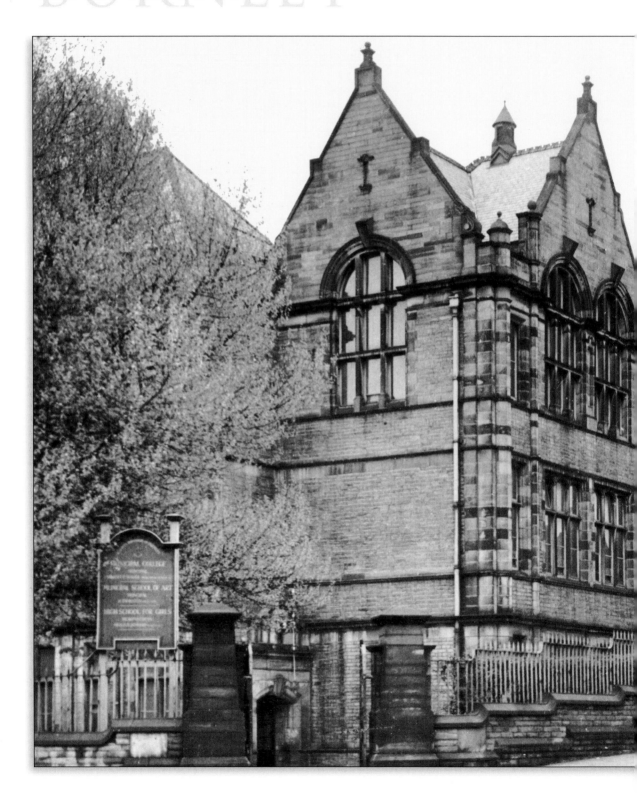

TOP O' TH' TOWN

Right: THE MUNICIPAL COLLEGE C1955 B251022

Below: DETAIL OF EWS SIGN

The original entrance to the college was intended to be from Ormerod Road, as the impressive doorway indicates. To the right are the trees of Thompson Park — it was fortunately among them that Burnley's only Second World War bomb fell. The street with the EWS (Emergency Water Supply) sign on the wall (the top edges of the letters are just visible bottom left in the Detail) is Shorey Street, which leads to the river. The Shorey Well was situated nearby.

DUKE BAR AND EASTERN BURNLEY

THE most important highways that serve the eastern part of Burnley can be seen in the photograph of Duke Bar as it was in 1906 (54183, right). The road to the left is Colne Road, and the one to the right is Briercliffe Road. In the centre is the Duke of York public house (c1882), and it is from this building that the first part of the local place name is derived. The second word, 'bar', is because these roads once formed part of an important turnpike. A toll bar, with gates across both roads, once stood here; hence the name Duke Bar. The roads lead the traveller in the direction of Yorkshire.

In the days when few people could afford a watch, there were many more public clocks. In Burnley they were placed at strategic locations across the town, and this one at Duke Bar certainly fits into the pattern.

DUKE BAR 1906 54183

The Duke of York is one of Burnley's landmark inns, and gives its name to this part of town. The tip of a spire can be seen just off centre. It belongs to St Andrew's church, which dates from 1867 and cost £5,000. St Andrews School, opened in 1866, is directly behind the Duke of York. On the right is Eastwood's musical instruments shop — it appears to be on Briercliffe Road, but it is actually at 119 Colne Road. The sunblinds protected the various instruments from sunlight.

DUKE BAR AND EASTERN BURNLEY

DUKE BAR AND EASTERN BURNLEY

THE DUKE BAR BOTTLE STORES 1906 54183c

As we can see, Thomas Bate's general store took its name from the fact that it sold the Burnley-brewed 'Grimshaw's Sparkling Ales and Stout', which were also supplied to the Duke of York. Mr Bate's shop has several interesting signs on the walls: Sunlight soap, Bovril and Fry's cocoa. Later the shop became the local office for the Burnley Building Society.

The same is true of the large gas lamp to the right of the public house. The people of Burnley call these lamps 'gawmlesses', because like this one they were always found in the middle of the road! If we look carefully, we can see the more usual and smaller lamps on both Colne and Briercliffe Roads.

The pedestrians going about their daily business enliven 54183 (pages 18-19). Notice the policeman near the gawmless lamp, the men near the Duke of York, and the children on the left. Also there are two vehicles visible, a coal cart on Briercliffe Road and a tram on Colne Road. The open-topped tram is quite a rarity for Burnley, because only a small number

operated in the town. Notice also the stone setts, which make up the road surface, and how they merge into each other at junctions.

Higher up Colne Road, though here it is called Burnley Road, we reach Reedley, or to give it its proper name, Reedley Hallows. In 1883 a visitor noted that 'there are several very respectable residences in the Township', but the area still needed a police station! Picture 54199 (below) shows it when it was still very new. E and W Parker had completed the building in 1905 at a cost of £11,000. It was designed to accommodate a magistrates' court and retiring rooms and offices for the County Police.

THE POLICE STATION AND MAGISTRATES' COURT, REEDLEY 1906 54199

An open-topped tram is on its way to Nelson, whilst a young man in an apron, probably a tradesman, is walking in the direction of Burnley.

Duke Bar and Eastern Burnley

Left: THE VICTORIA HOSPITAL 1906 54196

This photograph shows the Victoria Hospital after the construction of Thornber Gardens, which were laid out in 1897, the year of Queen Victoria's Diamond Jubilee, at the expense of the Mayor of Burnley, Alderman Caleb Thornber. Notice smoke rising from a chimney behind the building. This is a reminder that Burnley was an industrial town. Frith's photographs tend to avoid industrial views of the town.

Above: DETAIL FROM A CIRCULAR WARD, VICTORIA HOSPITAL 1895 35796

This shows the children's ward, left of photograph, and one of the circular wards. Notice the cattle in the foreground on the site of what became Thornber Gardens.

Duke Bar and Eastern Burnley

The eastern part of Burnley contained almost all our hospitals. The oldest was the Burnley Infirmary (54185, pages 24-25) which was designed as part of the Burnley Union Workhouse in 1876 by William Waddington. This one replaced an earlier infirmary in 1895, but the name was changed to Burnley General Hospital when ownership passed from the Board of Guardians to Burnley Corporation. After the Second World War, Burnley General Hospital was incorporated into the National Health Service; with many additions, it is now the main hospital in the Burnley area.

The Victoria Hospital (54196, pages 22-23), which was built on a site off Briercliffe Road in 1886, was Burnley's first hospital not connected to an institution. Again, the architect was William Waddington: he was responsible for the two circular wards (35796, page 23), which at the time they were built were considered to be the latest in hospital design. The wards were named Thursby and Butterworth after two of the most generous of the hospital's benefactors. However, the ordinary people of Burnley paid for most of the hospital's running costs out of their wages, and all sections of the community supported money-raising ventures for the hospital. These included Burnley's famous Hospital Cup, which was competed for by teams of footballers from workplaces throughout the area.

THE WORKHOUSE INFIRMARY 1906 54185

The architect of this building was William Waddington who designed quite a number of distinguished local buildings. This part of the building, which housed the offices, has an impressive entrance. Notice the two large lamps by the path. There were wards for the inmates, laundries, kitchens and other facilities normally associated with a workhouse. It was also known by other names, the Primrose Bank Institution and Moorfields.

24

DUKE BAR AND EASTERN BURNLEY

There had been a smallpox epidemic in Burnley in 1876, and four cottages opposite the entrance to the Workhouse were converted into a small isolation hospital. It was not until 1895 that plans were drawn up for a proper isolation hospital. These plans resulted in the opening of the Burnley Sanatorium at a site on Marsden Road above Burnley Lane Head in 1899 (54198, right). Originally the facilities were to include a scarlet fever pavilion, an isolation pavilion, a mortuary and a laundry. Extensions were built in 1902, but even these were not big enough, so another isolation hospital was built at Crown Point.

Sanatoriums were often built in the countryside, because it was believed that fresh air was good for the patients. This was especially true of hospitals catering for those suffering from TB. Burnley Sanatorium appears to be surrounded by fields, but the town was not very far away.

THE SANATORIUM 1906 54198

LANCASHIRE COUNTY MAP

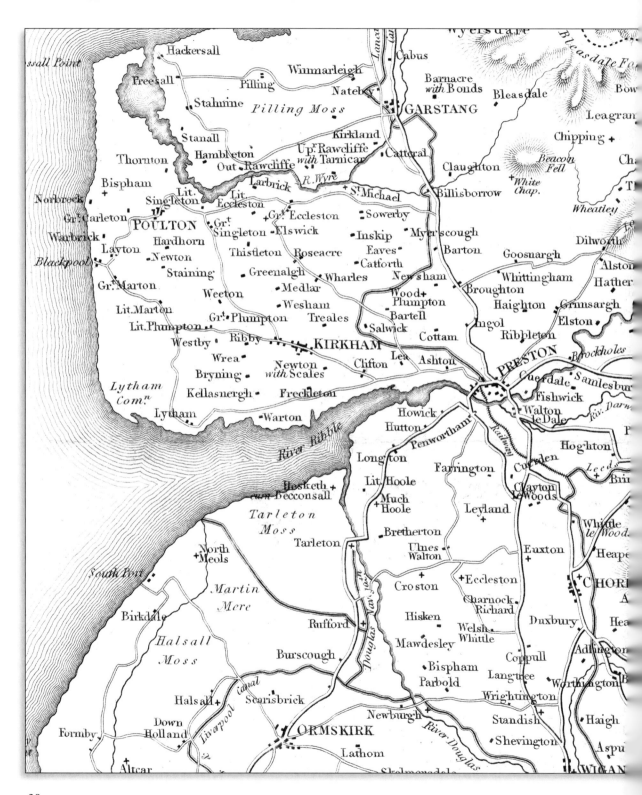

LANCASHIRE COUNTY MAP

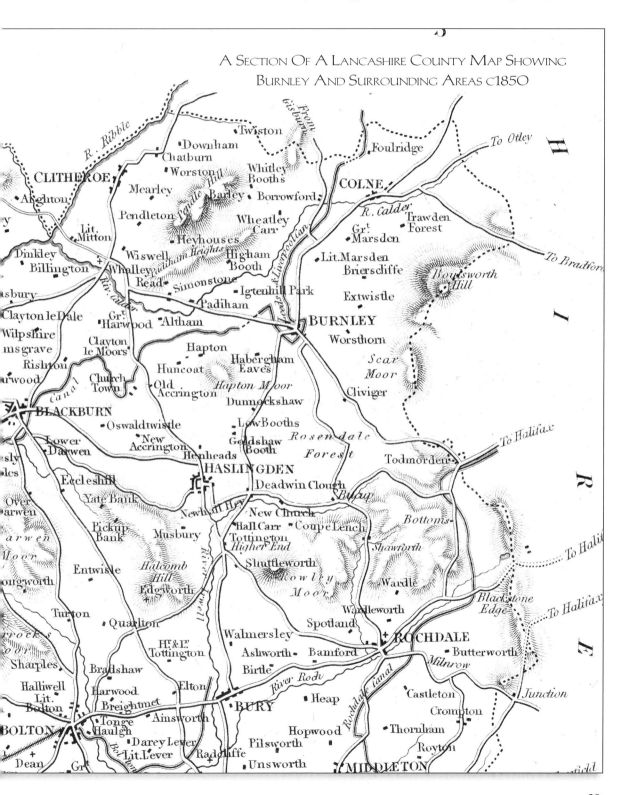

A Section Of A Lancashire County Map Showing
Burnley And Surrounding Areas c1850

BURNLEY

MANCHESTER ROAD

GIVEN its present importance to Burnley, it is surprising that Manchester Road is not one of the town's older highways. The direct route to Manchester followed by this road is a product of the early industrial revolution, and in fact even the name is relatively new. In the middle years of the 18th century the town centre moved from the Top o' th' Town to what became the junction of St James' Street and Manchester Road — except that neither of these highways was so called at the time!

Close to this junction was the 'merestone', which from 1819 marked the new centre of Burnley. The name for that part of what became Manchester Road nearest the merestone was originally Market Street, because the new Market Place was constructed there. To confuse modern Burnleyites, there is a Market Street Bridge, a reminder of the original name, on the present Manchester Road! Above the bridge the first name for the next section was Foundry Street, so called because of the location of the Lane Bridge Foundry. Then the next section of the road, as it climbs towards the moors which divide the Calder valley from the Irwell, was called South Parade.

THE TOWN HALL AND MARKET STREET BRIDGE 1895 35786

Perhaps the most noticeable change here would be that the ornate gas lamps have long since gone. The central dome dominates the building. However, it was originally intended that there should be a much higher tower with two flanking domes, but these were not built because some council members baulked at the cost. The façade of the Town Hall is perhaps too busy; but notice that it contains a number of niches. These were going to be filled with statues of Burnley's worthies, but again this project has not been completed.

31

MANCHESTER ROAD

MANCHESTER ROAD 1895 35789

This picture gives us a brief glimpse into the daily life of some of Burnley's people. Notice the woman, right, with the umbrella near the bollard at the top of Saunder Bank. In the middle of the road two young men, one with a bike, chat together. In front of them a little girl may have been asked to stand there by the photographer for the benefit of the composition, but one wonders if she is aware of what she is doing! The cart, left, was the usual way of carrying light loads around the town centre, but the carters often had difficulty on Manchester Road.

Photograph 35789 (above) looks along Manchester Road towards the town centre from just above the Market Street Bridge. We can see the bridge on the left near where two little girls in white dresses are standing; on the right, a line of small boys are sitting close to the other side of the bridge. Manchester Road nearest the town centre is largely given over to shops, and we will look at some of them in more detail, but at a later date, when we consider B251023 (page 39) and B251026 (pages 40-41). There is,

though, something worthy of our attention in the row on the right (the first shop is A Jackson's 'Baby Linen, Ladies and Children's Clothing (and) Outfitting Establishment') — this is the mast carrying telephone wire insulation pots, which can be seen on the roof. This reminds us that this building was Burnley's Post Office before the Hargreaves Street premises (54191, page 46) were built in 1905.

The buildings on the left of 35789 are the Town Hall and the Mechanics' Institute. On the right, the dominant building is the Brunswick Chapel. All three are the subject of separate photographs, but this one illustrates how the buildings appear in relation to each other and the rest of Manchester Road. It might also be worth pointing out the proximity of Nonconformity and the seat of local government. Methodists and Baptists were of considerable importance politically in Victorian Burnley.

Burnley Town Hall, with, to its right, the Mechanics' Institute (35786, pages 30-31) are perhaps the most impressive buildings on Manchester Road. Opened only seven years before the photograph on page 32 was taken, the Town Hall is an elaborate building (perhaps over-elaborate) in the Classical style; it does its job of dominating the Manchester Road very well. Inside, many of the Victorian features, including the large mosaic floors and stained glass, are intact. The ceiling of the Council Chamber, with its ornate plaster work and the frieze listing the Council's achievements, is perhaps the most spectacular feature.

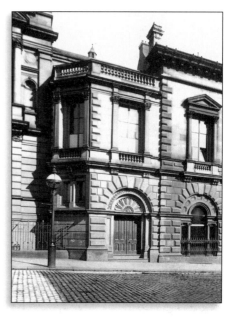

Above: THE MECHANICS' INSTITUTE 1895 35787

Top: DETAIL. THE MECHANICS' INSTITUTE 1895 35788

This is the new entrance to the Concert Hall, built in 1887.

MANCHESTER ROAD

Architecturally the Burnley Mechanics' Institute (35787, page 33), which is by the local architect James Green, is a much better building than the Town Hall. It dates from 1855, though in 1887 a new entrance (35788, page 33) was made to the Concert Hall, and a year later a new wing, once the Burnley School of Art, was added to the Yorke Street elevation. The large entrance with the four Corinthian columns (35787, page 33) is part of the original building, but the slightly compressed part of the structure, right, is the 1888 extension. Both the later extensions are by William Waddington.

Mechanics' Institutes had provided working men with educational and social opportunities unheard of before. This one served Burnley until 1959. Then, like many similar bodies across the country, a declining membership resulted in its closure. It had been competing with Council facilities, like the library and the college, whose services were often free. Afterwards, the building opened as the Casino Club, and since 1986, it has been Burnley's Arts and Entertainments Centre. The building is situated at the corner of Manchester Road and Yorke Street.

ADVERTISING AT THE MECHANICS' INSTITUTE
1895 35787C

At one time Burnley was described as the town with the most advertising hoardings in the country, probably because of rivalry between local firms. The hoardings generally inform locals about what is happening at the Mechanics', though there are commercial advertisements too. The three men are clearly more interested in the photographer from Frith.

MANCHESTER ROAD

Right: THE BRUNSWICK CHAPEL, MANCHESTER ROAD 1895 35800A

Though a good picture of a much-missed local landmark, this photograph also gives us a hint of Burnley as an industrial town. To the right of the chapel there are two large chimneys, with others in the distance. The near one is part of the Saunder Bank Ironworks, once the home of the Burnley loommakers, Butterworth & Dickinson. A little further away, and to the left, the next chimney may be at either the Burnley Gas Works or the town's Electricity Station. The latter had only just opened when this picture was taken. The other mill chimneys in the distance are in the Burnley Wood area.

Below Left: THE BRUNSWICK CHAPEL, THE INTERIOR 1895 35800B

Below Right: BY BRUNSWICK CHAPEL 1895 35800X

Caps, clogs and smocks: some of the clothes worn by children at this time.

MANCHESTER ROAD

Across from the Town Hall and the Mechanics' Institute, both of which are still in use, used to stand the Brunswick United Methodist Chapel (35800a, left) which was built between 1867 and 1869 at a cost of £10,000. The building was typical of many of the better Nonconformist chapels. Note particularly the Classical style of the structure, very different, and purposely so, to the Gothic of the Anglicans. To the right of the chapel some boys lean against Market Street Bridge, while two little girls have climbed on to its stonework and are hanging from its railings. The children can be seen more clearly in the delightful enlargement (35800x, below). Lastly, the magnificence of the Brunswick's interior can be seen in 35800b (page 36).

Higher up Manchester Road we come to the junction with Rose Hill Road (54187, page 38). This is an area of good residential property, as we can see from the bay windows and gardens. Members of Burnley's professional and business class — lecturers, large shopkeepers, the owner of a small brewery — and some retired people formerly in business, occupied these houses. This is the nearest one gets in Burnley to middle class suburbia; it is a very considerable contrast to the areas of town where the mill workers lived. The tram is probably on its way down Manchester Road. As the destination is shown as 'Towneley', it would have had to make its way via the town centre to Yorkshire Street and Todmorden Road and on to the terminus near Causeway End.

The tram would have had to pass close to St Matthew's church (35793, page 38) which dates from 1879. It is another building by William Waddington. The church we see in the photograph was largely destroyed by a fire which broke out on Christmas Day 1927. The church was rebuilt, and this time the contract went to the Lancaster firm of Austin & Paley: they had competed for the initial contract, but had lost out to Waddington's.

MANCHESTER ROAD 1906 54187

Space for trees in a street is often a sign that these were houses for the middle class. On the left the large trees are in Scott Park (54193, page 41).

ST MATTHEW'S CHURCH 1895 35793

For the last two photographs in this section (B251026 on pages 40-41, and B251023, below) we return to the junction of Manchester Road and St James' Street, but this time we are looking up Manchester Road rather than down. Another point to bear in mind is that there are about sixty years between the dates of the picture which introduced this section and the two that remain to be examined.

These pictures are a delight to those who are interested in old Burnley. They are representative of much that we have lost: though the buildings they inhabited have largely survived, the businesses — the shops, the inns and the offices — have now gone. It is also interesting to look at the people depicted in these photographs as they go about their business, most of them oblivious of the activities of the photographer from Frith. Look at what the men and women are wearing and what they are carrying, and wonder what issues of the day are on their minds or are being discussed in conversation. The vehicles — cars, buses (both Ribble and BCN) and even a motorbike and sidecar — tell their own story.

MANCHESTER ROAD c1950 B251023

This photograph was probably taken from a window in one of the shops on St James' Street. In the foreground is the Old Red Lion. Notice the little group of people chatting by the window to the left of the entrance. A shopper has placed a heavy burden on the windowsill. The building with the large dome is the Savoy.

MANCHESTER ROAD

*When this view was taken, Manchester
Road was a much more important
shopping street than it is today. On the
right, just above the Trustee Savings
Bank, is the New Day furniture store;
the building is now occupied by the
'Burnley Express'. On the other side
of Bull Street (right of photograph) is
the Big Window public house, one of
Burnley's best known inns, and in that
row were Bulcock's the ironmongers and
Bowker's the tobacconist. On the other
side of the road, the building with the
RAC sign was the Savoy Cinema, the
first in Burnley to screen a complete
sound film, 'The Singing Fool'. Beyond
the Midland Bank other businesses
included Shee & Kennedy's, Burnley's
principal tailors, the Café Royal and
Restaurant, and Kate Barnes, which was
well known for its ladies' gowns.*

BURNLEY FROM THE AIR 1955 AFR24732

CENTRAL BURNLEY

WHEN a passenger on one of the local Corporation buses asked for 'Burnley Centre', this was the intended destination. St James' Street (B251024, above) not only had many of Burnley's most well known shops, banks, public houses and cinemas, but this part of it also had the bus station. Unfortunately, only one bus is 'in' in the photograph. However, careful examination will reveal one of the large bus shelters beyond the patiently waiting crowd, which were provided for the use of the passengers on Burnley's all too frequent rainy days.

The view was taken at the junction of St James' Street and Manchester Road. The corner of the Old Red Lion is just visible, extreme right, and next-door is the Swan Hotel, perhaps the oldest building remaining in the

Even though it was obviously a busy time of day, it hardly seems necessary to have a Keep Left sign at this point. There is not nearly so much of interest on the left of the picture because of the bend in St James' Street. Originally, when this part of the street was known as Blucher Street, after the Prussian general at Waterloo, the bend was much more pronounced — it was known as Munn's Corner because of the business that operated there.

town centre. Originally a farmhouse in the early 18th century, it became an inn when the town centre moved to this spot a little later. The building enters local political history, because for a generation from 1816, it was here that the Town Committee met, the forerunner of the Council. Burnley's 'lockup', or prison, of 1819 is still situated behind the hotel; its small size, some say, is testimony to the lack of crime in those days, but also to the size of Burnley's population at the time.

As we move left there are a number of well-remembered firms on the row which begins with Martin's Bank

(right). The offices of Liverpool Victoria Insurance are above the bank. Just beyond Cavendish's, the furnishers, is the Clock Face Hotel: during alterations in 1910, an old clock was revealed above the door lintel. It is an early example of conservation, for it is believed that it was restored to its original position, despite the lack of working parts. Many will remember the Lubeck Milk Bar and the UCP (United Cattle Products) Restaurant. The latter firm specialised in the processing of tripe, but the restaurant here had a wide-ranging menu and was very good.

Left: THE GENERAL POST OFFICE, HARGREAVES STREET 1906 54191

This building exhibits all the usual features of a post office, including letter boxes, a clock and an information board giving details about collection times. The photograph was taken from Victoria Street. Notice the stone setts in the foreground, and the odd angle at which they are laid. The men and boys outside the GPO are very much aware that a photographer is at work. On the right, one man wearing a cloth cap and another a bowler are standing side by side. In the days when this photograph was taken, the type of hat worn often indicated status.

Below: ST MARY'S ROMAN CATHOLIC CHURCH, YORKSHIRE STREET 1895 35794

Two pubs come next, the White Lion, and on the other side of Parker Lane, the Boot Inn, but the word 'Stockdale's', emblazoned on the gable end of the next row, was like a magnet for many a young lad: Stockdale's was Burnley's premier toy shop. The row was designed in 1876 by the Padiham architect Virgil Anderton. Other businesses included Lupton's, the booksellers, Hesketh's, the cabinet makers and C F Hargreaves', the hardware merchants, who were better known as the 'Golden Padlock' because of the sign outside the shop.

On the extreme left of B251024 (pages 44-45) is Addison's, the wine and spirit merchants, and next to them the National Provincial Bank. Round the corner were the Palace, the Grand (both cinemas), the Public Health Office and Poole's silk shop. The clock was attached to the tram office. It was a famous local landmark, and became a popular meeting place for young and old alike.

The General Post Office (54191, page 46) was merely a year old when the photograph was taken in 1906. The

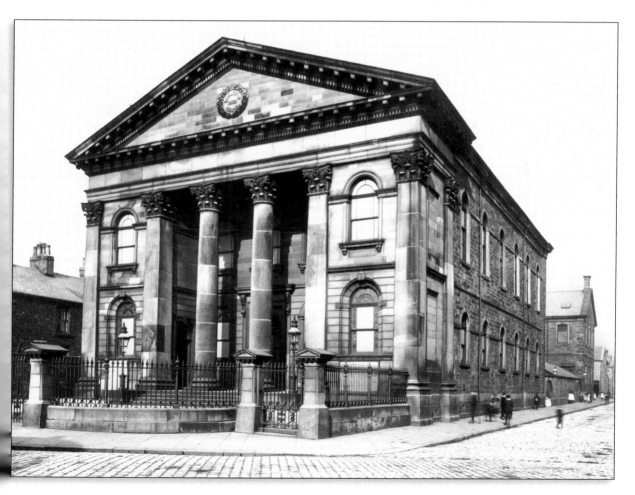

Fulledge Chapel, Todmorden Road 1895 35795

We can see the school for almost 400 pupils behind the chapel. In Eliza Street, a number of children are at play.

building is situated on Hargreaves Street, and it is constructed out of Huncoat brick and terra cotta with a granite base, an odd combination for Burnley. Also odd is the fact that it is built in the Flemish Renaissance style. Notice that the building carries a mast like the one we have already seen on Manchester Road (35789, page 32).

The Catholic church of St Mary, dating from 1849 (35794, page 46), dominates Yorkshire Street. Originally, the building was to have had an imposing tower and spire at the west end, but these were never completed; the result is that St Mary's, a fine building in other respects, does not look finished. Peregrine Edward Towneley of Towneley Hall gave the site, and the photograph includes the Towneley Chapel. This was built as a memorial to Richard Towneley, the last male heir, who died in Rome in 1877, and to his father, Col John Towneley.

Just around the corner in Todmorden Road stood the magnificent Fulledge Chapel (35795, page 46). It was built in 1860 for the Wesleyans in the Classical style so much championed by Victorian Nonconformists. The side elevations and the rear of the building were utilitarian compared to the front elevation. This consisted of five bays, with giant Corinthian columns supporting a pediment across the whole façade, creating a loggia, or arcade. At the back of the loggia there were several imposing doors into the chapel. Regrettably, after a number of years standing empty, Fulledge Chapel was destroyed by fire in 1990.

Handbridge Castle also stood on Todmorden Road (35800, right). It was not a real castle, of course, but the impressive entrance to the parkland which surrounded Towneley Hall — the castle was built in 1797-8 by Charles Towneley. The agents for the Towneley family used it for residential purposes; then it was purchased by Burnley Corporation in the 1920s, and after standing

empty for some time, it was demolished in 1958. Its name originated from a small footbridge with a handrail which used to take walkers over the Calder.

Rounding off this section, we come back to the town centre to consider photographs taken in 1961 of Burnley's Central Library (B251037, page 50) and its near neighbour the Police Station and Magistrates' Court (B251036, page 50). Both buildings are decorated with pennants because in 1961 Burnley was celebrating the centenary of its incorporation.

The Central Library is the building on the right of

HANDBRIDGE CASTLE, TOWNELEY PARK GATE, TODMORDEN ROAD 1895 35800

Charles Towneley, the 'great collector' as he is sometimes known, had plans for the housing of his collection of classical antiquities at Towneley Hall. Unfortunately, he died before this could be achieved, but part of his plan was to make improvements to the Park. Handbridge Castle was one of them.

B251037, page 50. The Earl of Elgin and Kincardine opened it in July 1930; it cost £37,500, of which the Carnegie United Kingdom Trust granted £16,000. The building behind was the head office of the Burnley Building Society when the picture was taken, and it, too, dates from 1930. The Lucas Group, the electrical engineers with several large factories in Burnley, gave the fountain in the foreground to the Council to commemorate the 1961 centenary celebrations, so it was very new when the photograph was taken.

When photograph B251036 (page 50) was taken in 1961, it was entitled 'Burnley, the New Police Station'. It was new because the building was opened in 1955 by the Rt Hon Gwillym Lloyd George MP, the Home Secretary. The photograph actually shows the part of the building occupied by the Magistrates' Court — the Police Station, only part of this building, is round the corner on Parker Lane. The site has had many uses; it has been a cattle market, a bus station for the long-haul services of Ribble, Hebble and Yelloway, and, of course, the fairground — also, the Gaiety Theatre once occupied part of the site.

CENTRAL BURNLEY

THE CENTRAL LIBRARY 1961
B251037

The Central Library is on Grimshaw Street. This photograph gives us the opportunity to look down the street and into Hargreaves Street, where the GPO stands (54191, page 46). In the background, the building in front of the mill chimney is part of the Hammerton Street central stores of the Burnley Equitable Co-operative and Industrial Society. The chimney itself is probably the one attached to the Co-operative building, which was once a foundry.

THE POLICE STATION AND THE MAGISTRATES' COURT 1961 B251036

The clock tower of Burnley Town Hall can be seen in the distance (right), and on the extreme right the Kwik Snaks café is visible. Those keen on classic cars might be interested to note that, left to right we can see a Morris Minor, a Morris Oxford, an Austin Cambridge, a Ford Consul and a Jaguar Mark VIII.

BURNLEY'S PARKS

BURNLEY is not a town known for its parks, but it should be. At the time of writing the Borough Council holds two Green Flags — the nationally recognised standard of excellence — for Thompson's Park in Burnley and Memorial Park in Padiham. Two other parks — Scott Park and Queen's Park — are being considered for Green Flag status, and it is hoped that the largest of the town's parks, at Towneley, will join them in the near future.

Burnley as a borough came rather late to the provision of this particular service. The reasons might include the fact that until the mid Victorian period, Burnley was a relatively small town. It might have been a smoky place in which to live, but no part of Burnley was very far from country lanes or the open moors, which can be seen from all parts of the town. In addition, Burnley already had several private parks and gardens. The owners often allowed at least occasional access to them. These included General and Lady Scarlett, and later the Thursbys, at Bank Hall, and the Towneleys at Towneley Park.

The town's first venture into the provision of open space fell short of the concept of the public park, but the recreation grounds that were provided were much appreciated. In 1872 Healey Heights, off Rosehill Road,

QUEEN'S PARK 1895 35798

The design for this park cleverly concealed a mineral railway line, which crossed the park from Bank Hall Colliery (owned by the Thursbys) to join the mineral tramway, which served Rowley Colliery. Queen's Park was laid out by Burnley Corporation, and it is a typical park of its time. There were two bowling greens and two children's playgrounds. The picture shows three buildings — the central one, a shelter, is still with us. To the right there is another shelter, but this has been removed. The small structure on the right was a bandstand.

Burnley's Parks

was taken at a 14-year lease, and by 1891 more land had been acquired at Wood Top, Burnley Wood, Stoneyholme and Lowerhouse. In 1893 Piccadilly Gardens and the Briercliffe Road Gardens were created. Two years later the Corporation acquired the Fulledge Recreation Ground, though this meant the closure of the Burnley Wood Recreation Ground, which had been sited near Towneley Station. By the turn of the century further recreation facilities were provided at Lanehead and St Andrews.

However, none of these facilities could be termed a public park. The first of these was opened at Queen's Park in 1893. Sir John Hardy Thursby had presented the land upon which the park was constructed to the town in 1888 as part of the celebrations of Queen Victoria's Golden Jubilee. Photograph 35798 (page 51) was taken only two years after Sir John performed the opening ceremony. Clearly, it shows Queen's Park in its very early days.

The next park to be opened was Scott Park in 1895. Alderman John Hargreaves Scott, a relative of the inventor of the spinning jenny and the owner of a watchmaker's business in Burnley, died in 1881. He left funds whose Trustees were charged with the task of purchasing land and laying it out as a park. In 1892 Burnley Corporation had secured the Hood House estate situated off Manchester Road, and it was here that Scott Park was developed. Picture 37405 (page 56) shows that those who planned the park made use of existing woodland, though more recent plantings can be seen to the left. Notice that some seats are arranged around mature trees. See also the sheltered bench to the right. Clearly those who designed the park were aware of Burnley's weather! Most Victorian public parks had bandstands, and the one we see in 54194 (pages 58-59) hosted many musical events. In the background new houses are being built, and there is a reminder of Burnley's cotton industry in the smoking mill chimney.

QUEEN'S PARK, THE KEEPER'S LODGE AND THE GATES 1895 35797

This picture shows the Ormerod Road gates from inside the park. To the right is the Keeper's Lodge. Notice that the gates are decorated with the town's coat of arms. This part of the park was detached when the modern Queen Victoria Road was built.

SCOTT PARK 1906 54193

This photograph shows Scott Park when the plantings had yet to come to maturity. The memorial is to the founder of the park. The park's layout indicates its ornamental nature.

Burnley's Parks

BURNLEY'S PARKS

Right:
A SECLUDED SEATING AREA AT SCOTT PARK
1896 37405

Below Left:
THE MEMORIAL TO ALDERMAN SCOTT IN
SCOTT PARK 1906 54192

Below Right:
SCOTT PARK, THE ORNAMENTAL FOUNTAIN
1930 B251004

*A natural stream passes through the park, and this
was made into a very pleasant feature.*

THE BAND STAND AT SCOTT PARK 1906 54194

BURNLEY'S PARKS

Towneley is often called 'the jewel in Burnley's crown'. It is not an inappropriate title. In this section of the book, we are restricted to the park; the Hall itself will come later. Towneley Park is the remnant (quite a sizeable one, as it is almost 250 acres in area) of a medieval hunting park. There is still a deer pond in the park. The first 62 acres were purchased in 1901 from the Dowager Baroness O' Hagan, the last member of the Towneley family to live at the Hall. A year later the park opened to the public, but it was not until 1925 that the major purchase, almost 174 acres, was made by the Council.

A park of 250 acres is big enough to be several parks, and so it is here. The land around the Hall, formerly the gardens, orchards and walled garden of the Towneley family, can still be identified. To the east is Thanet Lee Wood, which was planted by the family. At Higher and Lower Towneley are the football pitches and the municipal golf course, though a lot of Lower Towneley is now in the hands of the County Council because much of this land is used for school sports.

Charles Towneley probably designed the avenue (54203, opposite, above left) in the late 18th century as a feature of the woodland behind the Hall. The avenue rises to the Foldys Cross, which dates from 1525 and originally stood in the churchyard at St Peter's as a memorial to a chantry priest who died in that year.

The fourth of the parks to be included in this book, though there are more, is Thompson Park, which was opened in 1930. It is named after James Whitham Thompson, who was a cotton manufacturer in Burnley. The park occupies the site of the grounds of Bank Hall (35803 and 35804, page 69), but they were changed beyond all recognition by the landscape architects who designed the present park. Perhaps the two main features in Thompson Park are the Italian gardens and the boating lake—unfortunately, the Frith photographer did not take any pictures of the former.

Above Left: TOWNELEY HALL, THE AVENUE 1906
54203

Above: TOWNELEY, THE MUNICIPAL GOLF COURSE
c1960 B251044

*Five golfers on the municipal golf course at Lower Towneley.
The photograph looks in the direction of Causeway End and
Todmorden Road.*

Left: TOWNELEY PARK, THE WAR MEMORIAL
c1960 B251045

*Dating from 1926, the war memorial was opened by the
Earl of Derby, though its cost was borne by Caleb Thornber,
a cotton manufacturer and former Mayor of Burnley. The old
plantings around the memorial probably date from 1803; if
so, they are the work of Charles Towneley.*

TOWNELEY PARK, THE STABLES CAFÉ C1960 B251046

Left: THOMPSON PARK, THE BOATING LAKE C1955 B251028

This photograph shows the impressive footbridge which spans the lake, but it also reminds us that Burnley is an industrial town; the chimneys are those of the Burnley Brick and Lime Co Ltd, which had works at Heasandford and Queen's Park.

Below Left: THOMPSON PARK, THE BOATING LAKE AND THE REFRESHMENT ROOMS C1960 B251039

By the time this photograph was published, the popularity of boating had resulted in 'traffic regulations'! The chimney to the right is that of Park Shed on Leyland Road.

Below: THOMPSON PARK, THE BOAT HOUSE C1960 B251041

An idyllic scene: flowers in the foreground, the lake and the boat house against a setting of trees and shrubs — but the chimney of Bank Hall Colliery is a reminder that we are in Burnley.

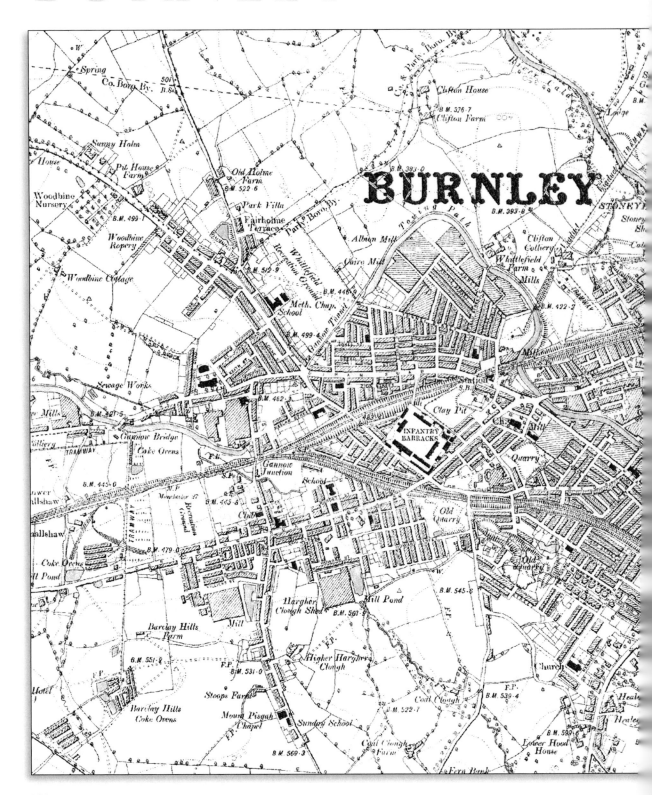

An Ordnance Survey Map Showing Burnley And Surrounding Areas 1891

BURNLEY'S HISTORIC HOUSES

WHEN people think of Burnley, more often than not it is of the football club and smoky factory chimneys that they think. This is understandable. The exploits of Burnley FC are widely reported in the media, both local and national, and the club enjoys much wider support than one might expect. To others, whether they have visited the place or not, Burnley is a typical northern industrial town. They mention the town's mills, its coal mines, its terraced workers' houses; some people expect to see dozens of flat caps and shawls on our streets!

Of course these things constitute a caricature of the town and its people, and as with most images arrived at without much thought, they are unhelpful and inaccurate. The truth is that Burnley is a town of many contrasts. It has its industrial estates, but the town is surrounded by attractive countryside. There are areas of older terraced property, but Burnley also contains residential districts that have Conservation Area status. In fact, Burnley has probably maintained closer links to its past than most industrial towns.

The town has preserved smaller relics: the 13th-century market cross in the Old Grammar School Gardens and the Foldys Cross from the 16th century at Towneley are examples. In addition, Burnley has Towneley Hall Art Gallery and Museum, and Gawthorpe Hall, which is owned by the National Trust and administered by Lancs C C. There are a number of other 'heritage' attractions, and we have seen that Burnley has an almost unrivalled record for the preservation of its Victorian parks. There is nowhere better in the north-west of England for local people to understand the town of their birth and its past.

An aspect of local history, not now as popular as it used to be, which is very well covered by Frith, is Burnley's historic houses. Most of the photographs date from 1895, and a surprisingly large percentage of the buildings survive. The images give us a glimpse of the days when the 'big house', and its family, dominated other people's lives. The dynasties which occupied these properties were in the main landowners, and their incomes were derived from the usual sources associated with the land-owning class. However, this being Burnley, those who had property were interested in commerce just as much as the manufacturers were. The landowners, for example, owned the mineral rights to Burnley's coal measures, and they also owned the land upon which mine buildings had to be built. A number of Burnley's land-owning families enjoyed large incomes from this source, and it is true to say that for one of them coal was especially important.

Overlooking the ancient centre of Burnley was Bank Hall (35803 and 35804, page 69). A half-timbered house occupied the site in the early 14th century, and at that time it was in the ownership of the Woodruffs. They remained there until the 17th century, when the property eventually passed to the Shireburns of Stoneyhurst. When that family died out in the male line, Bank Hall passed to the Welds of Lulworth, but in the 18th century the property came to the Hargreaves family. It was this family that owed its very considerable prosperity to coal, and it was after one of them that the Exors of Colonel Hargreaves, Burnley's largest coal firm, was named. In the 1830s the male line failed. One daughter of Col John Hargreaves married the man who was to become General Sir James Yorke Scarlett, and the other married the Rev William Thursby.

BANK HALL 1895 **Top:** 35804 **& Above:** 35803

There had been a house (probably half-timbered) at Bank Hall in the Middle Ages, but in about 1780 it was decided to improve the building, and the structure seen in the picture was the result. Bank Hall served as a military hospital in the First World War, and in 1919 it became Burnley's maternity and children's hospital. In 1895 the Hall was still in private hands. Note the window boxes in the top view and the bowed façade which overlooked Burnley.

CLIVIGER, ORMEROD HALL 1895 35805

This photograph shows the house with its two towers. The stable block is linked to the house by an archway (right). In the foreground an agricultural labourer is cutting hay, whilst another appears to be inspecting his work.

BURNLEY'S HISTORIC HOUSES

The Rev William Thursby went to live at Ormerod Hall, also known as Ormerod House (35805, pages 70-71), a magnificent house in Cliviger. The Hargreaves family had also owned this, but it had been in the occupation of the Ormerod family for centuries before that. The estate came into the possession of the Hargreaves family on the marriage of the heiress, Charlotte Anne Ormerod, to Col John Hargreaves.

Whilst we are in Cliviger, it would be as well to cover the other houses of that parish and its neighbour Worsthorne. One of the most charming of our local historic houses is The Holme (35809, opposite), which fortunately is also one of the most accessible, because it stands alongside the Burnley to Todmorden Road. The photograph was taken in 1895 when the house was still in the hands of the family which had lived there for centuries, the Whitakers. The plantings behind the house were the work of Dr Thomas Dunham Whitaker, who was awarded the Gold Medal of the Royal Society for this work and more on his estate. He is better known as an antiquary and one of the founders of the discipline we now call local history.

Also in Cliviger is Barcroft Hall (35811, pages 74-75). It became part of the Towneley estate, though it was for centuries occupied by the Barcrofts of Barcroft. It is an example of a smaller country house, and dates from the early 17th century. Two houses at Hurstwood are worthy of mention. Hurstwood itself is described by Pevsner as an 'architecturally rewarding hamlet'. It still retains its agricultural labourers' and handloom weavers' cottages, but it has a far more interesting history than that.

CLIVIGER, THE HOLME, THE HOME OF THE WHITAKERS 1895 35809

The Holme takes its name from an ancient Scandinavian word which means 'an island surrounded by marshes', but the oldest part of the house dates only from the early 17th century.

Barcroft Hall 1895 35811

This is a typical E-shaped house. Some have claimed that the design was a tribute to Elizabeth I.

Top: HURSTWOOD, SPENSER'S HOUSE 1895 35807

Above: HURSTWOOD HALL 1895 35808

This picture shows the rear of the property, a very fine example of an East Lancashire house of the later 16th century.

ROYLE HALL 1895 35816

This photograph shows the house to its best advantage. It stood in a delightful position in the years before Burnley started to expand into a modern town. In the latter part of the 19th century, Royle Hall was the home of Canon Arthur Townley Parker, the long-serving incumbent of St Peter's.

One of the properties there is Spenser's House (35807, page 76) and it is believed that the Elizabethan poet Edmund Spenser, the author of 'The Faerie Queene' and 'The Shepheard's Calendar', lived there when a young man. Only a few yards away is Hurstwood Hall (35808, page 76) which dates from 1579 and was built by Barnard Towneley.

For the next house we travel east of Burnley to Royle (35816, above). The property is first mentioned in 1296 as Rohille, which means 'the hill of the roe deer'. This is not surprising, because this area was at this time part of an important hunting chase, and later a forest belonging to the Crown. The house seems to have been in the occupation of the keepers of the park, and the family became known by their occupation as Parker. In the reign of Henry VIII, Royle became the property of a branch of the Towneleys of Towneley, though they changed the spelling of their surname, dropping the first 'e', to avoid confusion. The estate remained in their hands until 1796; but by a peculiar circumstance, the heiress of the Royle estate had married Robert Parker of Extwistle and Cuerden, and so the estates of these families were united.

The remaining houses belonged to the three most important families in the district. Huntroyde (35820a, pages 78-79) was the home of the Starkie family; they came to Simonstone, where Huntroyde Hall is situated, when Edward Starkie married Elizabeth Symondstone, the heiress of John Symondstone. This was at the end of the 15th century, but the oldest part of the present house, as it appears in the photograph, was built in 1576. A large park, called the Huntroyde Demesne (we see little of it here), surrounds Huntroyde.

Burnley's Historic Houses

Gawthorpe Hall (35818, page 80) is situated in Ightenhill, though most local people regard the property as being Padiham's most important house. The Hall has been associated with the Shuttleworth family since the 14th century, but the present building dates from 1600 to 1605 and is the work of the Rev Lawrence Shuttleworth. In 1850 Sir James Kay-Shuttleworth commissioned Sir Charles Barry, the architect of the Houses of Parliament, to restore the Hall. When this photograph was taken, the family was still resident; the fourth Lord Shuttleworth decided to move to Leck, though his aunt, Rachel Kay-Shuttleworth, lived here until her death in 1967.

The last of our historic houses, and the most well known, is Towneley Hall. The photograph dated 1906 (54201, page 81) shows the Hall only five years after it was purchased by Burnley Corporation from the last Towneley to live there, the Dowager Baroness O'Hagan. Towneley is first mentioned in a deed of c1200 when Roger de Lacy, the Lord of Clitheroe, granted Geoffrey, his son-in-law, two oxgangs of land 'in Tunleia'. It was this Geoffrey who was the founder of the Towneley family. He doubtless built a house in the area of the present Hall, probably to the south of Castle Hill, but it was not until the end of the 13th century that Towneley became the permanent home of the family. The present Hall dates from about 1400, and small parts from this period survive in both the south-east and north-west wings.

SIMONSTONE, HUNTROYDE HALL 1895 35820A

Medieval Towneley consisted of a great hall with two protecting wings, together with a fourth wing which created a complete quadrangle. It was this latter wing that was removed in the early 18th century to create the front elevations we now know.

Over the years so much work has been undertaken at Towneley that the story of the building is difficult to unravel. The 1930 photograph (B251010, pages 82-83) of the south-east wing clearly shows the diagonal buttresses and the turrets. One would like to believe that they are medieval, but they actually date from the 18th century, when it was fashionable to add features like these to existing buildings. It is likely that only some of the battlements are original.

The chapel (B251015, page 82) is a much-appreciated part of Towneley Hall. It was usual to have a chapel in a house of the stature of Towneley in medieval times, and we know that there was a chaplain there in the 13th century. The chapel dates from about 1515; it was built by Sir John Towneley as part of the wing which was eventually demolished in the early 18th century, and material from the original building was used to reconstruct the present chapel. The picture shows the chapel without the magnificent 15th-century Dutch altarpiece that was installed into the Hall by Charles Towneley, the famous art collector. Mary Elizabeth Towneley gave the altarpiece to the convent of Notre Dame at Ashdown Park, but it has been returned to Burnley.

IGHTENHILL, GAWTHORPE HALL 1895 35818

This photograph shows the gardens to the front of the Hall and the 'pele tower', which probably existed here in the Middle Ages. Behind the Hall the land falls away to the Calder.

This is the most well known view of Towneley Hall. It shows the building casting a reflection in the pond at the front. To the right, partly hidden by trees, are the former servants' quarters. Some visitors can be seen by the central door. What is often not realised is that another wing once stood here. It contained the family chapel, which was later moved into the west wing. The only things which spoil this view are the municipal benches.

TOWNELEY HALL, THE SOUTH-EAST WING 1930 B251010

On the top floor the south-east wing contains the long gallery; below it are what are now called the Regency rooms. The north-west wing, which can be seen in the background, contains the chapel, the kitchens and the two art galleries. In the foreground, the garden area to the left was originally part of the orchard. Note the woman with a child in a pram at the front of the Hall.

Burnley's Historic Houses

Right: TOWNELEY HALL, THE ART GALLERY c1955 B251019

Towneley Hall has a very good collection. It includes the famous Zoffany portrait, 'Charles Towneley and his Friends', several Turners and an Epstein bust. Most of the pictures have been acquired by the Council, though the Hall has some pictures formerly in the Towneley Collection.

Below: TOWNELEY HALL, THE CHAPEL c1955 B251015

The chapel is the work of Sir John Towneley (1473-1541), who also saved the magnificent vestments formerly used in Whalley Abbey. The vestments, very rare survivals of the pre-Reformation church, are usually on display near the chapel. The chapel itself is full of interest. On the extreme right, note the beautifully-carved wooden shield over the door of what was once a confessional room. On either side of it are the crests of the Towneleys of Towneley and the Asshetons of Lever, together with the initials RT and IT and the date 1601. The initials are those of Richard and Jane Towneley (formerly Assheton). High on the panelled ceiling are bosses on which are carved the initials of Sir John's family.

Towneley Hall, The Kitchen c1955 B251013

BURNLEY'S HISTORIC HOUSES

Towneley contains a magnificent kitchen; in B251013 (page 83) we see the spits in front of the fire and the range, which dates from about 1820. There are two art galleries (B251019, page 83) at Towneley. They date from 1924, and they occupy space which was originally bedrooms and the library. The last room we see is the long gallery (B251020, below). The long gallery was a most important feature of many old houses, as it afforded residents the possibility of exercise in bad weather. When the family was in residence, over one hundred portraits of Towneley ancestors filled the upper panels; the portraits dated from the reign of Elizabeth I. The displays had changed by the time the photograph was taken.

The long gallery is 85 feet long. It differs from other long galleries in that four bedrooms adjoin it. These were used as guest rooms. The panelling is 17th-century and the ceiling bears the initials of the Towneleys who lived in the late 15th and 16th centuries. At the north-west end of the gallery a door leads to a spiral staircase, long since sealed. This descended through the six-foot-thick wall to the chapel below.

TOWNELEY HALL, THE LONG GALLERY C1955 B251020

INDEX

The following people have kindly supported this book by purchasing limited edition copies prior to publication.

In memory of Ken Bolton

To Bill, a very good friend of Dad's, from Trevor and Jean

To Elizabeth, fond memories of Ken, from Trevor and Jean

In memory of Dad, from Trevor and Jean

To Christopher, in memory of Grandad, love Trevor and Jean

To Matthew, in memory of Grandad, love Trevor and Jean

To Jonathan, in memory of Grandad, love Trevor and Jean

To Gary, in memory of Grandad, love Trevor and Jean

To Carl, in memory of Grandad, love Trevor and Jean

To Jenny, in memory of Step-Grandad, love Trevor and Jean

Happy memories of Ken Bolton, Brenda Rochester

Thankyou Roger for putting this book together, June Rochester

Alec, a great achievement. Love Margaret x

As a tribute to my parents. Kenneth Allen

John Paul Alston

Mr & Mrs L M Andrew, Burnley

Linda Anforth

Peter F Ashkettle

Mr & Mrs H Ashworth, Evesham, Worcestershire

John Milton Aspden

Duncan James Aspden, love from Dad

Suzanne Claire Aspden, love from Dad

Avis and family, Jean, Colin, Gordon, Jackie

Trevor James Bailey

Robert and Shirley Baird

To my nephew Andrew Bamber, on his birthday

To my nephew David Bamber, on his birthday

To Pamela Barnes on her birthday

Ken & Marina Barrett, on their golden year

To Julie Barrett. Happy Birthday, Mum and Dad

Ken & Jean Barton, Auckland, New Zealand

The Bates and Stokes families, Ronald and Margaret

The Bates Family, Burnley

The Bates Family, South Africa

To Claire Bates on her 30th birthday

Mr and Mrs Benton

Mrs Mollie Berry

Geoff & Carol Billington

Stewart and Lucy Binns, 2006

To Tony Birchall and family, love Mum

Mr William Neville Blakey

To my brother, David Bland, on his birthday

Carol G Boothman

Anita J Boothman

Barbara A Boothman

Albert Bottomley

Jack and Dorothy Bottomley, Burnley

Ernest Bowes

Sheila Bowes

Roger and Jennifer Bramley

Happy Birthday Brian, love from Irene

John Brimblecombe

Michelle, Michael and Steven Brown, Burnley

In memory of Horace and Jennie Brown

Alan and Christine Brunskill

To William Burnie on your birthday

In memory, Jack and Christina Burrell

Kathleen and Donald Butterworth, Burnley

Anthony and Lynda Butterworth, Burnley

Elaine Butterworth, Happy Birthday, Mum

The Cambridge Family, Worsthorne

Simon & Nicola Capstick, Cliviger

Robert Cardwell, Bob, on his 70th Birthday

Pauline and Bryan Catlow

Happy Birthday Pat, 70, Les and Hilda Cherry

Bobby Claret, Burnley till I die

The Clegg Family

Mr and Mrs R Collinge, Daisy Bank Crescent, Burnley

Martin Collins, Burnley

Mr and Mrs C F Colton, Scott Park, Burnley

Michael P Conroy

The Cooper Family, Thornton-Cleveleys

The Cowgill Family

To my daughter, Judith Coyle

David S Crossley, Burnley

Malcolm and Janet Crossley, Burnley

The Cruz Family, Harle Syke, Burnley

Mr & Mrs Eric Cunlisse Hartley

Irene Cunningham

Joanne and Kyle Currie

Dad, a small thank you for all your help, Andrea

Dalian, Courtney, your roots explained. J B

Peter and Jean Darby, Golden Wedding

To John Davies, Burnley, on his birthday

Mr John Dean, Burnley

Back to my roots, Barbara Devitt

Amelia Dicioccio

In memory of Carol Donnelly, Burnley, 2005

In memory of Mr & Mrs W J Duxbury, Burnley

Brian Edmonson

Happy Birthday Elsie, love sister Avis

For the Emmett Family of Burnley

Francis William Ensor

A and M Fenton

Mr & Mrs M J Fitzpatrick, Lowerhouse, Bly

Mrs J Foster

In fond memory of Frank and Elsie Foster

Remembering the Fosters and Franklands

From Joan to Frank

The Greaves Family, Briercliffe

To my Dad, George H Green. Love Shirley

The Haigh and Whittaker Families, Burnley

David and Janet Hall of Cliviger

Sandra and Jennifer née Halliday

T Haney as a gift to Mum, A Percival

Mr & Mrs K J Hare, Burnley

Mr and Mrs H Harris, Cliviger

The Harrison Family, Burnley

Mr & Mrs Tom Harrison, Warton

To our son, Arthur Harrison, Burnley 2006

To our son, Keith Harrison, Burnley 2006

To Ann Cheryl Hartley. Love from Mum

Nigel Hartley and Family, Burnley. From Dad and Mum

Trevor Hawke

Raymond Haworth

To Irene Hayhurst, all my love, Steve

Eric and Joan Hebdon and grandson Sam

Mrs M Helliwell & sons, Keith & Colin, Burnley

Stephen Hepworth

Mr & Mrs P Hicks and son, David Hicks

Kim Joseph Hillam

Mr & Mrs Brian and Mary Hirst, Barrowford

In memory of John Holden, Burnley

In memory of Ian Robert Holgate

The Hollingworth Family, Rimington

Mike & Rita Holsgrove

The Holts. Ian, Marie, Laura, Liam. 25.03.06

Karen and Alex Holtum

To George Hough on his 80th Birthday

The Howley Family

Mrs M Hutchinson and son Richard

Dr Keith Ingham

Mr & Mrs B Jackson, Burnley

The Janowski Family, Burnley, Lancs

Joan Kennedy

Muriel B Jobling, Burnley

John & Sonia, Burnley

The Jordan Family, Burnley

Joyce & Cliff, 'Some forgotten but happy days'

Judith & Jemma, with love Robert xx

Charles Leslie Kerrigan

Our parents Eleanor & Clifford Kershaw

King's Mill Antiques, Harle Syke, Burnley

The Knowles Family, Burnley born and bred

To Grandad Lancaster, Happy Birthday, love Thomas,
   Laura and Katie xxx

Stephen Latham

Christine Lee

Mr Donald Leeming, Brierfield

To Lesley and Nicki, the loves of my life.

To Leslie, best wishes, Dad

William R Lewis, in memory of Renne Lewis

Gary Lewis, for his 50th Birthday, Sheila

To my sister Linda, from Susan

Peter John Lister - your home town

Maureen Lockwood, Habergham Eaves, Burnley

Mr Ronald Lomas

Philip and Janet Lombard

Linda and Geoffrey Lord

The Lord Family, Burnley

To Lynda on your 40th birthday, love Dad

Lynne, Sarah, Anna, Poppy, Ned

In memory, Bernard and Irene McKavett

Helen Lewis & Luke Maddox, Burnley

To Marjorie, from Alan on her birthday

To Mum Sylvia Marshall, Happy Birthday, Bly

Pauline Martland

David Mason, Burnley 2006

Ellie, Katie and Isabel Maudsley

John Miller

To the memory of Mavis Moffitt

Hubert K Moorhouse

Peter James Morris

Peter and Cynthia Morris, Burnley

As a tribute to my parents, DJ Murray

Philip Graham Myers

To Nanna Mary on her birthday

Mr & Mrs Roger Naylor, Burnley

To Ken Neilson, on your 57th birthday

In memory of Norman, from Mick & Margaret

To my father Bernard Nuttall, love Sharon

Mrs Vera Nutter

Lee and Morgan O'Sullivan, Burnley

To daughter Pamela, love Mum xx

The Patten Family, Burnley

Paula & Keith, on your 30th, love Mum

To Dorothy and Bill Pemberton, from the family

Eileen Pickles

Denis Potts and family, Burnley

Fred Poulton

Harold and Doris Reaney

Mr Ronald Redfern

For Susan Riley - in memory, Burnley

John and Shirley Riley, Ightenhill

The Roberts Family, Burnley

To Alan Roberts, love from Ashley & Katie

Terence Robinson, Burnley

Kathleen Robinson

From Peter and Enid, to Ronnie with love

Best wishes to Rosalind, Matthew, Lindsey, Adam and Anthony

From Rose and the grandparents

Ann Royle

Maureen Ryder

Mr & Mrs E and P Sagar

Love and thanks to Sandria and Hugh. Mum

Edna Saul and children, Ian and Linda, Burnley

Doctor Craig Sayers

Andrew J Scholes, Cliviger, Burnley

Mr and Mrs John Scott

Mr & Mrs J Shackleton

Carole Shutt, Stuart L Walton, Royle Lodge

Mr & Mrs H Shuttleworth. In memory of our parents

Remembering Bill and Annie Siddall

Harry & Lily Singleton

To Derek Slater for his birthday

John Smale

Martin Richard Smith, Burnley

As a tribute to my grandad, Allen Spencer

In memory of my father, Harry Spink

Ian F and Marjorie Stacey

Mr & Mrs C Stanworth, Briercliffe

In fond memory of Harry and Ida Stanworth

Mr and Mrs L Stevens

Carol Stinton

Christine Stockdale

In memory of my husband Ray Stokes. Trudi and family

Graham McDonald Storey

To Bertha and Ken Stott, special friends.

Jack Sunderland

Beryl Sunderland

To Susan, from Dad, with love

William A Suthers, a very special grandad

Dennis Taylor of Burnley

Mr & Mrs J Taylor of Harle Syke

Mrs Joan Taylor, Wall Stream, Worsthorne

Sue & David Taylor, Worsthorne, Burnley

To the Taylors, NZ. Love the Williamsons

The Thoburn Family, as a tribute for 35 years of marriage

Peggy Ada Thompson, née Smith

Yvonne & Terry Thorne, Old Hall Farm

The Thornton family, Harle Syke

To Ray Threadgold on his birthday

Alan Threadgould

Tina, Rod and family, from Burnley, 2006

To my husband Tom, with my love, Joyce xxx

John C Tomlinson, Burnley. For Prof Alan

Allen Nigel Tomlinson

Bob & Sue Tomlinson, Overtown, Cliviger

Andrew and Alison Tomlinson

Rob Waddington, Burnley

Mary Wainscott

Anne & Ken Walsh

To Mum, Jean Walton, for her 70th Birthday

Charles & Margaret Walton. Tribute from Irene

Carol Ann Ward 24/07/45   Jeffrey Ward 1/5/45

Mr & Mrs S Wells and family, Mereclough

Mr & Mrs Wheadon, married 55 years on 26th March 2006

Margaret and Neil Whitaker

John Whitefoot

Remembering William Whitham. The Clark Family

Mr & Mrs A Whittaker, Burnley

Gillian Wilkinson

The Wilkinson Family, Burnley

Mr P L Wilkinson, Burnley

The Wilkinson Family, Burnley

Martyn David Williams, on his birthday

Haydn Spencer Williams, on his birthday

Mr John Wills, Bly

Stuart & Susan Wilson, Ightenhill, Burnley

Vera Wilson

Malcolm and Ann Wiseman

The Wood Family, Nelson

Christine and Stephen Woodruff

Margaret J Wooller, Huffling Hall, Burnley

Florence Kay née Wormwell

Thanks Rob, for forty happy years, love Barbara

Wendy Wright, Burnley

Michael, June, John and Sarah Wright, Burnley

John Wright

Mr Ian J & Mrs Margaret Wrigley, Burnley

Stella Yates

FRITH PRODUCTS & SERVICES

Francis Frith would doubtless be pleased to know that the pioneering publishing venture he started in 1860 still continues today. Over a hundred and forty years later, The Francis Frith Collection continues in the same innovative tradition and is now one of the foremost publishers of vintage photographs in the world. Some of the current activities include:

Interior Decoration

Today Frith's photographs can be seen framed and as giant wall murals in thousands of pubs, restaurants, hotels, banks, retail stores and other public buildings throughout the country. In every case they enhance the unique local atmosphere of the places they depict and provide reminders of gentler days in an increasingly busy and frenetic world.

Product Promotions

Frith products are used by many major companies to promote the sales of their own products or to reinforce their own history and heritage. Frith promotions have been used by Hovis bread, Courage beers, Scots Porage Oats, Colman's mustard, Cadbury's foods, Mellow Birds coffee, Dunhill pipe tobacco, Guinness, and Bulmer's Cider.

Genealogy and Family History

As the interest in family history and roots grows world-wide, more and more people are turning to Frith's photographs of Great Britain for images of the towns, villages and streets where their ancestors lived; and, of course, photographs of the churches and chapels where their ancestors were christened, married and buried are an essential part of every genealogy tree and family album.

Frith Products

All Frith photographs are available Framed or just as Mounted Prints and Posters (size 23 x 16 inches). These may be ordered from the address below. From time to time other products - Address Books, Calendars, Table Mats, etc - are available.

The Internet

Already ninety thousand Frith photographs can be viewed and purchased on the internet through the Frith websites and a myriad of partner sites.

For more detailed information on Frith companies and products, look at these sites:

www.francisfrith.com

See the complete list of Frith Books at:
www.francisfrith.com
This web site is regularly updated with the latest list of publications from The Francis Frith Collection. If you wish to buy books relating to another part of the country that your local bookshop does not stock, you may purchase on-line.

For further information, trade, or author enquiries please contact us at the address below:
The Francis Frith Collection, Frith's Barn, Teffont, Salisbury, Wiltshire, England SP3 5QP.
Tel: +44 (0)1722 716 376 Fax: +44 (0)1722 716 881 Email: sales@francisfrith.co.uk

See Frith books on the internet at www.francisfrith.com

FREE PRINT OF YOUR CHOICE

Mounted Print
Overall size 14 x 11 inches (355 x 280mm)

Choose any Frith photograph in this book.
Simply complete the Voucher opposite and return it with your remittance for £2.25 (to cover postage and handling) and we will print the photograph of your choice in SEPIA (size 11 x 8 inches) and supply it in a cream mount with a burgundy rule line (overall size 14 x 11 inches).
Please note: photographs with a reference number starting with a "Z" are not Frith photographs and cannot be supplied under this offer.
Offer valid for delivery to one UK address only.

PLUS: Order additional Mounted Prints at HALF PRICE - £7.49 each (normally £14.99)
If you would like to order more Frith prints from this book, possibly as gifts for friends and family, you can buy them at half price (with no additional postage and handling costs).

PLUS: Have your Mounted Prints framed
For an extra £14.95 per print you can have your mounted print(s) framed in an elegant pol-ished wood and gilt moulding, overall size 16 x 13 inches (no additional postage and handling required).

IMPORTANT!

These special prices are only available if you use this form to order. You must use the ORIGINAL VOUCHER on this page (no copies permitted). We can only despatch to one UK address. This offer cannot be combined with any other offer.

Send completed Voucher form to:
The Francis Frith Collection, Frith's Barn, Teffont, Salisbury, Wiltshire SP3 5QP

CHOOSE A PHOTOGRAPH FROM THIS BOOK

Voucher for **FREE** and Reduced Price Frith Prints

Please do not photocopy this voucher. Only the original is valid, so please fill it in, cut it out and return it to us with your order.

Picture ref no	Page no	Qty	Mounted @ £7.49	Framed + £14.95	Total Cost £
		1	Free of charge*	£	£
			£7.49	£	£
			£7.49	£	£
			£7.49	£	£
			£7.49	£	£
			£7.49	£	£

Please allow 28 days for delivery. Offer available to one UK address only

* Post & handling		£2.25
Total Order Cost		£

Title of this book . . . .

I enclose a cheque/postal order for £ . . . . made payable to 'The Francis Frith Collection'

OR please debit my Mastercard / Visa / Maestro card, details below

Card Number

Issue No (Maestro only)   Valid from (Maestro)

Expires   Signature

Name Mr/Mrs/Ms . . . .
Address . . . .
. . . .
. . . .
. . . . Postcode . . . .
Daytime Tel No . . . .
Email . . . .

ISBN 1-84589-131-7   Valid to 31/12/08

Free Print – see overleaf

Can you help us with information about any of the Frith photographs in this book?

We are gradually compiling an historical record for each of the photographs in the Frith archive. It is always fascinating to find out the names of the people shown in the pictures, as well as insights into the shops, buildings and other features depicted.

If you recognize anyone in the photographs in this book, or if you have information not already included in the author's caption, do let us know. We would love to hear from you, and will try to publish it in future books or articles.

Our production team

Frith books are produced by a small dedicated team at offices in the converted Grade II listed 18th-century barn at Teffont near Salisbury, illustrated above. Most have worked with The Francis Frith Collection for many years. All have in common one quality: they have a passion for The Francis Frith Collection. The team is constantly expanding, but currently includes:

Andrew Alsop, Paul Baron, Jason Buck, John Buck, Jenny Coles, Heather Crisp, David Davies, Natalie Davis, Louis du Mont, Isobel Hall, Chris Hardwick, Julian Hight, Peter Horne, James Kinnear, Karen Kinnear, Tina Leary, Stuart Login, Sue Molloy, Sarah Roberts, Kate Rotondetto, Eliza Sackett, Terence Sackett, Sandra Sampson, Adrian Sanders, Sandra Sanger, Julia Skinner, Lewis Taylor, Will Tunnicliffe, David Turner and Ricky Williams.